BIRDS
of
POINT REYES

BIRDS
of
POINT REYES

Keith Hansen

Heyday, Berkeley, California

Library of Congress Cataloging-in-Publication Data

Names: Hansen, Keith, 1958- author.
Title: Birds of Point Reyes / Keith Hansen.
Description: Berkeley, California : Heyday, [2023]
Identifiers: LCCN 2022041747 (print) | LCCN 2022041748 (ebook) | ISBN 9781597146036 (hardcover) | ISBN 9781597146104 (epub)
Subjects: LCSH: Birds--California--Point Reyes National Seashore--Identification. | Bird watching--California--Point Reyes National Seashore. | Point Reyes National Seashore (Calif.)
Classification: LCC QL684.C2 H36 2023 (print) | LCC QL684.C2 (ebook) | DDC 598.072/3479462--dc23/eng/20220923
LC record available at https://lccn.loc.gov/2022041747
LC ebook record available at https://lccn.loc.gov/2022041748

Cover Art: Pelagic Cormorant (front) and Rock Wren (back) by Keith Hansen
Cover Design: Diane Lee and Marlon Rigel
Interior Design/Typesetting: Marlon Rigel

Published by Heyday
P.O. Box 9145, Berkeley, California 94709
(510) 549-3564
heydaybooks.com

Printed in East Peoria, Illinois, by Versa Press, Inc.

10 9 8 7 6 5 4 3 2 1

To the late Rich Stallcup, a pioneer in California birding, an inspirational mentor, a loving father, a gifted author and wordsmith, and a germinating seed to myriad environmental causes

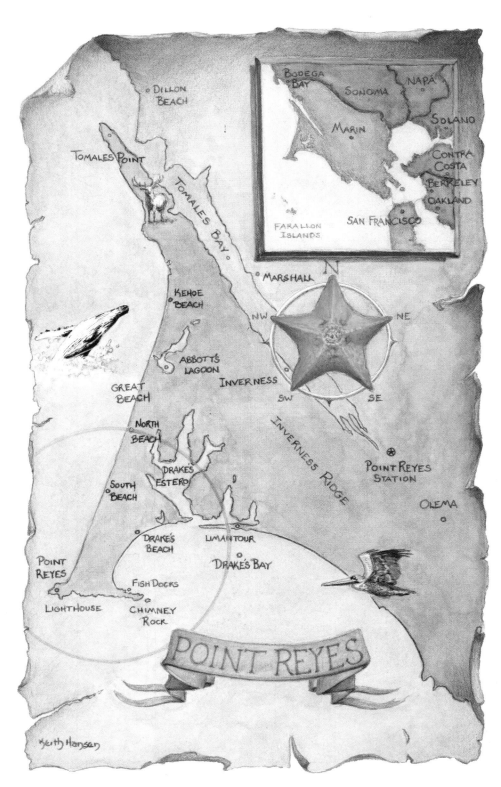

Contents

Introduction

If the lure of discovery while cradled in the embrace of wide-open spaces beckons you, birding might become a portal through which you find a deeper relationship with nature.

Were someone to ask me to describe Point Reyes, I'd likely find myself pausing for a moment and feeling somewhat perplexed as well as endlessly inspired. A smile would doubtless find its rightful place, and I would probably look way off into the distance and consider the sweep of the question. Point Reyes is one of those exceptional places on Earth that can be regarded and revered from a broad array of perspectives.

Vantage Point Reyes

Consider Point Reyes through an artist's brush, a photographer's lens, a poet's verse. Regard the myriad ways one perceives, envisions, or assimilates what is essentially a limitless resource of inspiration. Into eyes, through minds, down hands, becoming lines—the result of perception combined with craftsmanship is expressed as art.

With the long-term view of a geologist, you might reflect on this strikingly sculpted and distinctly shaped land mass. In awe, you would certainly consider the massive tectonic forces that rotate the Pacific Plate counterclockwise. Moving northwest over tens of millennia, the Point Reyes peninsula *races* along at a rate of almost two inches a year, or about thirty-two thousand years per mile. The Pacific Plate's eastern edge grinds smooth the western periphery of North America's great continental plate, creating the infamous San Andreas Fault.

Ask a mammologist! Inspiration comes in many forms, so brace yourself to be regaled with a hundred distinct stories of a hundred different species that call the Point Reyes National Seashore their full-time home, an annual destination, or their personal seafood restaurant. They range from the tiny vagrant shrew, weighing almost as much as three pennies, to the colossal blue whale, at over one hundred tons. Marine mammals of flipper and fin patrol offshore waters or glide through sun-spangled shallows. Elephant and harbor seals haul out onto beaches to battle, breed, or rest. On foot, herds of tule elk again roam the outer reaches of the peninsula. Over hill and dale, mule deer, river otter, badger, bobcat, and mountain lion please the eye and thrill the heart.

For the scientist, Point Reyes offers a rocky, ocean-pounded, weather-scrubbed classroom with elemental forces as its curriculum. It's a place where the meteorologist, the oceanographer, and the geologist can meet each time that wind drives waves into cliffs.

Few locations on the California coast have a greater vantage point than the outer tip of Point Reyes. Here the picturesque lighthouse clings precariously to the last hope of land before the Pacific becomes all-encompassing. I've always viewed Point Reyes not only through my binoculars, telescope, or camera but through the lens of *all things avian*. This peninsula, varied and wondrous, has it all. Stop, look, and listen. You'll see birds, perhaps not always, nor everywhere, but if you're observant and explore, or better yet find a quiet place, one with a lofty view, chances are you'll be rewarded with feathered magic.

You know, this might be the perfect place to begin, so!
Let's get to the point!

A Quick Look Around

Leave North America's continental plate behind. Drive out past the small picturesque towns of Point Reyes Station and Olema. Step west over the threshold of the San Andreas Fault, and wind northwest along Tomales Bay, through fir- and oak-shrouded Inverness. Climb over the forested slopes of Inverness Ridge and meander down an alder-lined creek. Emerge out and onto an open coastal plain, with a view that stretches from horizon to horizon. From North Beach and beyond ... you will have entered the area covered by this book: the outer point.

On a clear day, stand at the tip of Point Reyes. Scan miles to the north—Bodega Head protrudes southward, while eighteen miles due south, the Farallon Islands rise up like a seafarer's nightmare or a biologist's dream. Southeast, even further, you can see beyond the rugged cliffs of southern Marin to the streets of San Francisco. From clifftops, scan surging swells hundreds of feet below and scope far out, west or south. Whether floating on the water, diving beneath its surface, migrating a few feet above it, or wheeling high overhead, a myriad of seabird species can be encountered on the ocean, no matter its tempestuous mood.

In acutely discourteous weather, birds seeking salvation find refuge beneath wind-twisted cypresses that dot the outer point. These oases provide safe, dark roosting habitat for owls and cover for disoriented migratory songbirds to rest in after having been lost at sea. The protective cypresses and pines at Drakes Bay's fish docks provide birds sanctuary from biting cold and stinging wind.

The high cliffs bordering Drakes Bay create a bulwark that structurally protects the bay and shelters the waters surrounding the fish docks from strong northwest winds. Here, seals haul out on long sandy beaches. Offshore seas may roil; however, conditions here are often calm, even downright placid. On slowly rolling swells, seabirds rise into view and descend.

Stroll grassland or rolling hill dotted with lupine and scan for soaring, coursing, or hovering hawks. In these sweeping grasslands, stay alert as sparrows, larks, and pipits may take wing from underfoot. In winter, gregarious flocks of Western Bluebirds mixed with Yellow-rumped Warblers work fence lines. Unaccompanied, phoebes do the same.

Any trip to the coast is surely enhanced with a barefooted stroll along a sandy beach. Point Reyes is fittingly bookended, up coast and down, by long strands where shorebirds methodically chase waves in search of burrowing invertebrates. In drier habitat, the type beach ball–toting humans frequent, the Snowy Plover endeavors to raise its young in the sand's upper reaches. Upcoast from Point Reyes's tip, the exquisitely formed and aptly named Great Beach lies yawning for miles like a flawless necklace strung taut between the foundation of Tomales Point and the tip of Point Reyes. The natural pearls of South Beach, North Beach, and the seasonal inlet of Abbott's Lagoon all decorate this California treasure.

Downcoast from the mouth of Drakes Estero lies Limantour Spit. Boasting wispy beach grass and curvaceous windblown sand dunes, this unfailingly scenic strand is frequently alive with birds. Pounding waves create a rhythmic cadence to this lovely beachscape. Face the sea and look past perfectly formed breakers for the dorsal fins of Bottle-nosed Dolphin and Harbor Porpoise as they roll through gentle swells. Scoters, grebes, and loons ply waters beyond. Behind, Limantour Estero serves as a backdrop. Hand shaped, the inlet of Drakes Bay hosts a gathering of American White Pelicans who bide their time preening, associating, and resting.

From the historic US Coast Guard fish docks, out to Chimney Rock, and across the weather-worked face of the peninsula, the surf-battered intertidal zone is largely inaccessible. However, you can gaze down on it from clifftops high above. Welcome to the wet and wild world of the oystercatcher, Sea Lion, cormorant, and murre, where gulls patrol the shoreline utilizing updrafts for an effortless commute, free from flapping. Piercing the surf's dull beat, sweet trilling riffs cascade down the cliffs, courtesy of a singing Rock Wren. Pocked with holes, this vertical world of wind and rain-scoured cliffs provides nesting accommodations for the Peregrine Falcon. Feathered fare in abundance and updrafts created by driving winds afford this scimitar-winged sky pilot unlimited dominion over Point Reyes.

Perhaps low-lying short grass is your passion. Found near the turnoff to Drakes Beach and in a few other locations, this seemingly featureless habitat offers opportunities for Pacific

Golden-Plovers, longspurs, and even the endearing Burrowing Owl. Ranches with Holstein or Angus, as well as "*Homo sapiens*-enhanced" areas, are magnets for great flocks of blackbirds, starlings, and pigeons. Patiently filtering through these multitudes can sometimes reveal unusual species drawn to the congregation. Watch for ravens who swoop, zoom, or flip upside down with heart-stopping barrel rolls.

Several freshwater (and some not-so-freshwater) ponds are dotted here and there. Ponds at Mendoza and Spaletta Ranches offer habitat for various migratory shorebirds and pond ducks. At Drakes Beach, marsh-loving birds inhabit cattail and mire. This is one of the few locations at the point for this productive habitat.

Seemingly limitless, a "habitat" not often considered: the sky! Give it a frequent glance. At one time or another, nearly every bird adorning Point Reyes (except for perhaps California Quail) has had to reach it through the sky. Scan far off, search nearby, look behind you, browse clouds, shield the sun with your hand, and listen for flight calls from above. Crowning you at all times, this vast sphere may harbor a species you might not otherwise encounter in any previously mentioned habitat. A bird far from its preferred domain may not care to descend earthward, preferring to continue unnoticed, in plain sight, high in the sky. Someone with a field of regard that lies from, say, Earth to treetop level may be missing a cornucopia of avian encounters. Stay attuned for swirling swifts, geese on high, or lofty kettles of hawks. A famous birder once said, "Don't be blissfully unburdened by awareness": look up!

The Clock and the Calendar—Timing's Everything!

People frequently ask, "What's the best time to look for birds?" Well, the best time of day, every day, is as early in the morning as possible. After sleeping or migrating all night, birds need to replenish fat reserves and replace lost fluids. As the morning warms toward midday, birds often settle down for a much-needed avian siesta. Before sunset, as temperatures decrease, foraging usually resumes. When temperatures are cool, or downright cold, birds with high metabolisms, especially insectivores, can be active all day searching for leggy prey on the ground or hidden under bark. Garnering the sufficient nutrients for survival and, ideally, gaining weight takes the investment of active foraging. Birds who are discreet in their movements and mindful of their surroundings are more likely to see another day. They take all due caution not to become food themselves to predators such as hawks, owls, or bird-eating mammals. Fluttering and flitting about, or exposing itself while drinking water, can put any bird at risk.

If your question is "What's the best time of *year*?"—that depends. Although summer is the season with the lowest diversity of species, the peninsula bustles with large numbers of breeding murres, cormorants, and gulls. Frequently sizable feeding spectacles occur offshore as great numbers of seabirds profit from the Pacific's bounty. In August, fall's southward migration begins as millions of birds pass over and around Point Reyes. Usually first to arrive are shorebirds from the Arctic, with a large percentage being juveniles on their life's maiden voyage. A wide array of land birds and songbirds pass through in September, with birds of prey increasing in number by October. In November, waterfowl and sparrows settle in. The winter months of December to February boast great birding even as the weather ranges from mild to severe. Well over two hundred bird species have been recorded in the annual Point Reyes Christmas Bird Count. Windy springs from March to May bring back a welcome rush of life, color, and warmer temperatures with northerly migration and the onset of the nesting season. Migrating northward from the tropics, boldly patterned songbirds either pass through or arrive to breed for the summer.

Going from Point A to Point B, but Ending Up at Sea

Many highly migratory land birds found at Point Reyes do most of their traveling at night, flying several hours—some birds, even for days. Whether correcting a navigational error or having become a wind-tossed by-product swept out to sea by the capricious nature of our climate, land birds will strive to make it back to the coast. Exhausted and absent solid earth, a migrant will gladly use a fishing boat for salvation. Weary birds might view Point Reyes, jutting far out to sea, as an outstretched hand, a lifesaver hewn from rock. Here they might rest, feed, and perhaps even . . . persevere.

Most of these sojourners seek refuge in the cypresses and surrounding habitat. These feathered travelers have covered great distances either along their usual migratory route or rather by accident; this latter group can be thousands of miles from their normal range. Discovering a rare species *can* cause a stir in the birding community. Primarily in spring and fall, "treasure seeking" birders can be found beneath these trees, gazing upward.

The Point Reyes Peninsula can be viewed as a jumping-off point for migratory birds ascending into celestial skies or, for an exhausted waif lost at sea, its last hope. The peninsula is a crossroads, a sort of Grand Central, and the skies above, a starry artery. For as long as birds have been traveling, a few hundred species have commuted along these atmospheric pathways used by untold millions of birds on their way to untold billions of destinations, near and exotic.

Before You Go—Respect

Before grabbing your binoculars and heading out to Point Reyes, be mindful of the families and folks who work there or call it their home. Their farms are often busy. Use caution around livestock and heavy machinery. Park safely, away from working farm activities. When birding near homes, be respectful of privacy, moderate your volume, and the like. Afford birds the space needed not to feel threatened. Observe; do not disturb. Barn Owls, for instance, roost in the cypress groves and, if flushed into the open, are vulnerable to predation by larger birds of prey. Pay attention to the cues birds give, and respond accordingly.

Power Tools

Enhance your birding experiences with a nice pair of binoculars, a good spotting scope, and a sturdy tripod. Stay with known brands. Choose optics offering an aligned, sharp, and bright image clear to the edge of the view. They should focus closely and be waterproof, sturdy, and comfortable in your hands. Many birding apps include images and vocalizations of birds. Some enable you to record sounds. Acquire a good field guide. If you're bringing along a notebook, include a line about the weather conditions. Note helpful new field marks, be they patterns, shapes, or behavioral traits that help you to arrive at a correct identification. List the birds seen and heard, as well as the total number of each. Informative as well as creative, field sketches can be profoundly helpful.

Be Prepared, Helpful, and Trustworthy

Before visiting a new birding location, familiarize yourself with the various species you're likely to see. Learn their habits, habitats, and seasonality, and how frequently they occur. Listen online to their songs and calls. In the field, if someone's in need, lend a hand. If they can't locate a bird or might benefit from a useful field mark, consider helping them out. If you spot a rare bird, validate the sighting with notes, a description, additional observers, or photographs. Admit identification mistakes. Everyone makes them; it's part of learning. If you are unsure of an identification, alert people. Spread news of the sighting and say those six and a half wonderful words: "I'm not sure what it is."

Locating Birds

Now that we've talked about locations and seasons, you have an idea of where, and when, to search for birds at Point Reyes.

What's the difference between encountering more species, versus viewing birds better? For most birders, finding large numbers of species in a year, a day, or an hour bestows both fun and glory. There are also those who prefer to take it a bit slower, scanning each branch and probing every bramble. A birding friend refers to these different styles as skimming versus digging. Skimming is covering as many habitats as possible as quickly as possible, to garner the most species. While certainly effective, it's exhausting, and comes with a larger carbon footprint. Digging, by contrast, focuses your attention on a smaller area, where you uncover species, often hidden ones, not typically found in the frenzy of skimming.

Keep your eyes to the skies, scan offshore, check fenceposts, treetops, telephone wires. Mind clouds, scrutinize movements in brush. Look at each individual bird in a flock. Soon you'll discover similar-looking but uncommon species. Note unusual interactions between birds. This can signal the presence of predators, food sources, or something else. Listen for and try to learn birds' calls, songs, and unique vocalizations.

Getting a Look

Often the best way to see birds is to stand very still and simply listen. Keeping your voice low increases your and other naturalists' chances of hearing faint birds. Much of the birding experience revolves around first hearing and then seeing the vocalizing bird. It's often better to wait until the bird moves to get a look. Remain quiet. Limit dramatic or sudden movements. Birds are attentive to unusual actions. Allow birds to comfortably reveal themselves to you. Perfect the art of standing still and be rewarded with more intimate and memorable encounters with the creatures of nature.

If a bird is perched against a bright sky, position yourself so that something dark is behind the bird, be it a tree, mountain, or building. Having the sun at your back or side offers better illumination of your subject. Bright sunlight bleaches out colors, causing birds to appear paler. Overcast conditions offer truer hues. The visual differences—and therefore the quality of your observation— between a bird in bright sun versus overcast can't be overstated.

Identifying a Bird

If the subject of your attention is in view, keep your eyes on it. Study the form, pattern, and colors. Look for striking traits, while also paying attention to the subtle. Focus on the bill, face, and legs. Note the bird's behavior, one of the surest clues to identification. How's it acting? Is it social, sedentary, or quietly foraging? Is it vocalizing? Can you record or photograph it? (Have a cell phone? Take a shot!) Study unknown birds for as long as possible. If the bird flies, quickly get your binoculars on it. Note wing pattern, tail shape, and flight style. Focus on what tree or which part of the field it descended into. Then get closer. Take notes, *then* refer to a field guide. Endeavor to get other naturalists onto your find and enjoy the pleasure of sharing your bird.

Barn Owl

SPECIES

Northern Harrier

Circus hudsonius
Fairly common—Resident
18″–22″ (female larger than male)

From all points east, make your way out onto the Point Reyes peninsula and enter the spacious living room of our first species, a predator of wide-open coastal grasslands. Northern Harriers work their territories by coursing low over rolling terrain. Deep, languid flaps are interspersed with rocking glides. Wingtips swept upward, these raptors can pivot rapidly, float moth-like, momentarily hover, and continue . . . until they make an instantaneous pounce using lethal, lanky, lemon-yellow legs.

While all birds of prey have excellent hearing, the Northern Harrier comes equipped with a facial disk shaped like that of an owl. Faint sounds, whether created by squeaking shrew or mischievous mouse, are guided toward ears attuned to such subtle vibrations.

Many birds of prey are specialists, focusing their dietary needs on a narrow selection of prey items. For example, Osprey feed exclusively on fish; accipiters and Merlin, almost entirely on other birds. Harriers, by contrast, are generalists. They feed from a wide menu, limited only by what reveals itself or flushes up before them. Harriers preferentially hunt small rodents, but prey items include various birds, snakes, and frogs—even large insects are *fare* game.

Females and males of most birds of prey appear very similar, even identical. Adult harriers, however, are strongly dimorphic, bearing little resemblance to their mate. Heavily streaked, the females are brown above and whitish below, pearl-gray males are blushed brownish, and immatures of both sexes are warm cinnamon brown. While usually silent, harriers infrequently utter a rapid series of coarse, agitated *chirk, chirk Chirk, CHIRK, Chirk, chirk* notes. They also give repeated, peevish, rubber-ducky squeals that rise and drop in one second, *piSS-EE-YOU! piSS-EE-YOU!*

Top to bottom: two adult males, adult female, immature male, and juvenile

Sparrows of Point Reyes

See Bird Group Species List for individual species

Most visitors to Point Reyes understandably beat a quick path to one of the many charismatic sights this peninsula offers, be it the stately lighthouse, battling elephant seals, or herd of noble elk.

Most anyone would settle somewhere between oblivious and indifferent when it comes to a little brown bird perched on a barbed-wire fence. Yet much of nature's true beauty lies deep in the appreciation of the subtle. And what could be more subtle than a sparrow? Understated beauty comes in many forms. Walk the rolling grasslands cradling swales of bush lupine and coyote brush. This habitat makes up large portions of the outer point, and in fall and winter, it's often loaded with sparrows. For denizens of this terrestrial domain, brown suits are always in style, and pin-striped? Even better! Take your time, focus in, and get to know winter's sparrows.

The color and pattern of dry grass, Savannah Sparrows are frequently encountered in large numbers in short stubble. Their yellow brow, fine breast streaks, small tail, and pink legs all are important marks. Frequenting brush, the larger, less gregarious wood-brown Song Sparrow is longer tailed, and heavily streaked below. It gives a dry sneezy *SMEW!* call. Discovering the furtive Lincoln's Sparrow takes patience, stealth, and sharp ears. It's patterned like a Song Sparrow with delicate streaks, a buffy whisker and breast. Listen for its distinct *BzzzzzzziT!* note. Forming the nucleus of mixed flocks, Crowns make an appearance. Seasonally common, both White-crowned and Golden-crowned Sparrows occur. Hear a loud *SMACK!* note? Watch for a large, usually single chocolate-brown sparrow, profusely marked on the breast and underparts—the Sooty race of Fox Sparrow.

Top to bottom: Savannah, Song, Lincoln's, and Fox

Turkey Vulture

Cathartes aura
Common—Resident
26″–30″

Some visitors to Point Reyes ask with excited wonder, "What are these great black birds? Are they eagles?" While certainly nowhere near the most numerous bird at Point Reyes, the Turkey Vulture, our friendly funeral director, is frequently encountered and frankly quite hard to miss.

Roosting in natural bonsai twisted cypress, vultures shuffle their wings, sending the night's dewy droplets in a thousand directions. When it's too early for warmth and the sky far too gray to offer anything approaching a thermal, they wait. Patience is their virtue, along with a ridiculously keen sense of smell and stomach enzymes that well serve these undertakers' purposes. After two days in a tree, a vulture's spirit and body would surely be lifted if it just had some heat.

Eventually, from the northeast, clear blue sky comes calling as illumination increases and shadows form. Fellow morticians take note and shuffle about, finding the room needed to spread wide their great black and silver panels. Vultures are a sort of living, breathing, solar receiver cloaked in blackish-brown feathers. Resilient, they can sit for a few days in dour conditions, but when warmth is applied, they come into their own. Uplifting things happen for vultures when the heat is on!

Vultures' breast muscles, unlike hawks', are not well developed. Consequently, vigorous flapping to gain altitude is not their preferred manner of ascending—employing rising columns of warm air is. Thermals afford them effortless lift high above Earth, to search for all manner of carrion.

The next time you glance skyward at one of these teetering, sun-powered, gentle giants, remember there are many places on Earth where great black soaring birds are not a daily occurrence.

Below, at rest: adult (*left*) and immature (*right*)

Black Phoebe

Sayornis nigricans
Common — Resident
7"

Say's Phoebe

Savornis saya
Uncommon — September to March
7.5"

New World flycatchers (Tyrannidae) represent the largest family of birds on Earth, with well over four hundred species. At Point Reyes in the winter, this enormous family is represented by just two species, the Black Phoebe and the Say's Phoebe.

Phoebes find prominent perches from which to hunt. With active head movements, they watch for passing insects. Spotting a prey item, be it fly, moth, or bee, they give chase, pursuing with exceptional dexterity. Sometimes unsuccessful, frequently fruitful, they worry the captured prey against a wire or branch and then consume it whole. Somehow a day at the outer point wouldn't be complete without exchanging glances with at least one, or better, both phoebes.

While Black Phoebes are occasionally found in drier habitat, they're very much "water flycatchers." Comfortable around humans, this well-tailored black-and-white friend is drawn to habitat with moisture. Whether your trails find you at a willow -lined creek, a cattle pond, a soggy gulch, or pounding surf, you will likely come across one or more of these active aerialists. Their typical calls include a strident, down-slurred *PSEW!* They also give a burry, downward, two-note *Seets-seeeeer*.

Now, make your way out and into drier habitat, colored in warm earth tones, with vistas as big as all outdoors. Next, wander. Wander widely. At some point, your meandering thoughts may be gently interrupted by a soft-sounding, drawn-out, mournful sigh. Moments later, the down-slurred *pieeeeeer* is usually repeated. Check wire fences, bare twigs, and earth mounds. This tan-and-cinnamon vocalist can often be surprisingly close by. Say's Phoebes are not only earth flycatchers but sky flycatchers as well, often hovering, pirouetting after, or vigorously pursuing insects, high into the air.

Surf Scoter

Melanitta perspicillata
Common—September to May, otherwise occasional
20″

Voluntarily garnering much of your caloric intake from beneath the turbulent waves that endlessly crash and roil over sandy beaches takes a certain kind of rugged. It just might be that some birds have it a wee bit rougher than others. Birds like the Surf Scoter.

Along the rough and ragged edge of Northern California's coast, where land, sea, and sky collide, only hardy creatures immerse themselves in this zone of high disturbance. Here, neoprene-skinned *Homo sapiens* are powered by the confluence of these great natural forces and glide effortlessly through liquid portals. Below them, invertebrates and soft-bodied worms are exposed and vulnerable to capture. With an oversized Picasso-esque bill, scoters crush and consume this wide array of prey.

Moderated by the ocean, weather conditions along the coast of Northern California are often quite tame. At other times . . . not so much! When powerful winter storms hit, seabirds seek refuge in the lee of land masses that afford them protection. Highly gregarious, scoters congregate, forming large rafts numbering into the dozens. Here, birds ride out the rough seas, squalls, and winter's long nights. It's easy to admire a bird built like the Surf Scoter, which handily weathers the hardships the Pacific's climate throws at it.

Away from breeding grounds, scoters rarely if ever vocalize. However, when they take flight, listen for a rapid "tooting" created by the leading edge of their wings. Over water, the loud *toot-toot-toot-toot* from its quick flapping carries great distances. In spring migration, long sinewy strands containing hundreds of scoters move north en route to breeding grounds in northern Canada and Alaska. The sheer number of birds can astonish.

In flight: male (*above*) and female (*below*).

Common Raven

Corvus corax
Common—Resident
22″–24″

Any big black bird at outer Point Reyes that's not a vulture is almost certainly a Common Raven. American Crows are all but nonexistent here, and young eagles are infrequent, and immense. Greater than a Red-tailed Hawk in wingspread, bill-to-tail length, and weight, ravens are North America's largest species of songbird! They are a true passerine and one of the few capable of gaining altitude on a thermal without flapping. They soar!

Birds of legend and lore, ravens can seem larger than life. Supremely skilled a-wing, they appear to test the limits of speed, forces of gravity, and certainties of inertia. The inherent finesse of this corvid's artistry in flight, its sheer brazenness against all manner of hawk and eagle, is admirable. Vocalizing loudly while flipping upside down or executing a complete barrel roll, ravens are spirited daredevils. On long wings, swept down and back, ravens appear as if they're sliding on ebony blades, gliding on invisible ice. Along with Peregrine and Red-tail, this jet-black aerialist largely holds dominion over the skies above Point Reyes. While crows are usually gregarious and associated with humans, ravens tend to be loners. Singles, pairs, or small family groups are the norm. However, in the fall at the point, very occasionally, large numbers of ravens assemble into imposing flocks, sometimes massing into lofty spirals.

For better or worse, ravens profit greatly from the actions of, or unnoticed side effects from, humans. Food is garnered through picnic theft, dumpster malfunction, or nightly roadkill. Smart, shrewd, and calculating, ravens flourish. A skewed increase in intelligent, motivated predators can have negative effects. Where ravens occur, predation increases on all birds, especially ground-nesting species like Snowy Plovers.

Ring-billed Gull

Larus delawarensis

Common—September to May, uncommon summer

17″–18″

There's a bumper sticker floating around some birding circles that reads, "I don't DO Gulls!" Understandably frustrating, gull identification can seem bewilderingly complex. Not only plumages but also leg and bill colors differ depending on age.

Simply highlighting a couple of important traits can help with an overall understanding of gulls. Smaller species reach maturity in one to two years; larger species can take up to four. There's a remarkable "stair step" in sizes for the nine regularly occurring species on Point Reyes, ranging from the smallest, the Bonaparte's Gull, to the largest, the Glaucous-winged. Immature gulls are dingy in color with dull bills; as adults they become whiter headed, yellow billed, and blue-gray backed. When mature, every large species has pink legs. None of the medium or small species do. Rather, their legs are greenish, black, or yellow, as in Ring-billed Gulls.

This common species, the Ring-billed, might just open a portal of greater understanding and appreciation for this large and fascinating tribe. While most gulls mix freely with other species, Ring-bills tend to be a little standoffish, often roosting away from, or at the edge of, large gull gatherings.

Rather small, the Ring-billed Gull occurs from coast to coast. Whether they're chasing waves on sandy strands in coastal Florida, floating above harvesting tractors in America's heartland, pilfering french fries from an asphalt sea, or resting on Drakes Beach at Point Reyes, you *have* seen these pale-backed, yellow-eyed gulls. Shrewd, and through staring eyes . . . they've seen you as well! Calculating, they'll quickly size up your value as a potential provider of unattended food. Quick look right, and your potato chip left.

Point Reyes Spring Seabird Migration

See Bird Group Species List for individual species

Get a good pair of binoculars, a quality scope, and a sturdy tripod. Next, find yourself at the tip of Point Reyes in April, the height of spring migration. Get out early, sunup if possible. Dress warmly—it can be downright windy. Commit time. It doesn't happen all at once. Nail it on the right day, and you just might witness one of California's most dramatic natural events. Spring migration has a narrow calendar window; thus higher numbers of birds pass on individual days. Fall migration is spread out in duration and so appears less well defined.

Perfect for these moments, the outer point comes equipped with a spacious observation platform providing an unsurpassed vantage point. The sheer number of birds that may pass from left to right in a few hours can boggle the mind.

As if on parade, thousands of Pacific Loons, many in breeding plumage, fly northward. Skeins of murres come and go, some landing at their colony below. Western Grebes sprinkled over the swells are sometimes joined by the less frequent Clark's, Eared, Horned, or Red-necked Grebes. Great flocks of Brant wend by for nesting grounds in northern Alaska. Test your birding skills on passing gulls. It's not unusual to see half a dozen or more species in the mix. Pigeon Guillemots with their flashing white wing patch make identification simple; distant shorebirds are more challenging. And scoters! Jeez! Strand after strand, infrequently with White-winged Scoters or Harlequin Duck, join the commute.

So run your eyes along each twisting black necklace to see what might sparkle. Lastly, keep your eyes and mind open. One never knows what life-enhancing avian treat might pass your way on an April day.

Top to bottom: Pacific Loon, White-winged Scoter, Harlequin Duck, Western Grebe, Horned Grebe

Black Oystercatcher

Haematopus bachmani
Uncommon—Resident
17''

Look and listen for Black Oystercatchers at the rockiest edges of Point Reyes's intertidal zone. Supremely camouflaged, they all but vanish against wet stone. While they frequent the extensive boulder-strewn shores of the outer peninsula, they're certainly never in numbers.

Sharp and ringing, their strident proclamations pierce the Pacific's roaring surf. Nimbly avoiding surging walls of spray, approaching oystercatchers herald their presence, coming across loud and clear.

The species name would imply that these hardy birds consume oysters, but the Black Oystercatcher seldom if ever does. In pairs or small groups, this crow-sized shorebird comes equipped with a seemingly luminescent, scarlet-orange blade of a bill. Long, straight, deep, and laterally compressed, this "organic Swiss Army Knife" comes in handy for this shorebird's varied diet. The myriad tasks demanded from a tool of this sort are impressive. Whether chiseling mussels from beds, teasing small crabs from crevices, or popping limpets from rock, oystercatchers are deft and handle their bills adroitly. Young birds exhibit a dusky outer half to their bill, thereby softening the clashing contrast exhibited by adults. As if to visually balance the adults' dazzling red mandible, Black Oystercatchers come equipped with thick, sturdy legs of bubblegum pink.

Ear catching and eye seizing, an aerial display often begins as an entertaining, if not downright comical, showy flight over roiling surf. Usually two clamorous birds move about, vocalizing vociferously and flapping with shallow, modified, quivering wingbeats. Landing with wings momentarily open, both birds quickly throw their heads downward, their sizable bills almost touching rock. Raising their tails skyward, they proceed to let out a loud, long series of ringing notes that culminate in a laughter-like staccato.

Pigeon Guillemot

Cepphus columba
Fairly common—March to September, otherwise rare
14″

Perhaps originally named because of its exaggerated head movements and sturdy pigeon-like shape, Pigeon Guillemots are not, in fact, related to pigeons. Rather, they're in the auk family (Alcidae), which includes murres, murrelets, puffins, auklets, and the extinct Great Auk. So let's gaze out to sea and . . . talk auk!

To find this midnight-black and snow-white seabird, scan waters off the fish docks, or scope out to sea from clifftops on the outer point. Exclusively a saltwater inhabitant, guillemots occur fairly close to rocky coastline, becoming less numerous farther from land. Birds usually float in small rafts of a dozen or fewer, where they gather and dive in search of food. Underwater, whether in pursuit of sculpin or juvenile rockfish, guillemots "fly" using their wings for propulsion.

Pigeon Guillemots are clearly able to discern guillemots of the opposite sex; to humans, however, they appear identical. Their motif is bold and strikingly patterned. First encounters can be arresting. Fall juveniles, by contrast, appear rather scruffy gray and white with pale grizzled patches to the head, back, and wing coverts.

Unlike murres, who nest in bustling colonies numbering into the thousands, guillemots nest singly or in rather small groups and clusters. Pairs lay their eggs on narrow cliff ledges, within crevices, or on human-made structures such as piers and pilings. On a blur of wings, nesting birds approach rapidly, emitting a high, thin, nearly inaudible, descending *TS,s,s,s,s,sssssss* whistle.

Nimble afoot, they run up cliffs or over rocks on astoundingly red feet, frequently holding their fluttering wings high overhead. Resting birds lie flat on their bellies, concealing their feet. When birds vocalize, look for the contrasting crimson mouth lining.

Snowy Plover

Charadrius nivosus
Common—October to March, otherwise uncommon
6.5″

Whether it's the bird's cheerful *TioooweeP?* call, its ability to run astoundingly quickly over dry sand, or its unobtrusive, low-profile demeanor, this rather large-headed plover is utterly endearing. And their two or three chicks? Few things on this Earth are as cute. Fluffy as a dandelion, they're snowy white below. Above, they're the color of dry beach sand sprinkled with tiny, dark particles.

In wide-open conditions, well above the beach's curvaceous high-tide line, Snowy Plovers nest among shell fragments, twisted driftwood, and a whole lot of dry sand. Frequenting several locations at Point Reyes, these sand-colored plovers are slowly, but thankfully, increasing in population.

Sadly, for Snowy Plovers, life hasn't always been a day at the beach. As we've developed the California coastline and taken over sandy beaches with houses, roads, and invasive plants, they've struggled to survive. Turmoil from summer beach activity, off-road vehicles, off-leash dogs, looming drones, and the robust presence of human-adapted predators such as ravens, raccoons, gulls, and coyotes ensures a challenging life for *any* beach-nesting creature.

Like Snowy Plovers, we *Homo sapiens* like nice warm beach sand under our feet. All good! However, to protect the sensitivity of their breeding areas, please frequent beaches not reserved for nesting plovers. There are plenty! Respect protective fencing around spring and summer nests. If, while walking a lonesome beach, you do find an unprotected nest or encounter these birds roosting in the nonbreeding season, always observe from afar.

The fate of this kindly beachcomber will surely improve if we all steer clear of their remaining nesting areas.

Below, left to right: juvenile, male, and female

32

Double-crested, Brandt's, and Pelagic Cormorants

See Bird Group Species List for individual species

Although cormorants are most closely related to pelicans and boobies, they can resemble a loon when floating, a goose in flight, or a vulture drying outstretched wings in the sun. They are wedded to water, or the land adjacent to it. Here at Point Reyes, we are endowed with three species.

Most folks familiar with cormorants have likely cut their teeth on the Double-crested. The most frequently seen species occurring inland, they're encountered widely across the US. Nesting, they build rickety platforms high in trees in several locations in Marin County, typically at bustling heron rookeries. Large numbers enjoy lounging on the railings at the Point Reyes Lifeboat Station at the fish docks. When migrating or covering greater distances, they often assemble in goose-like V formations. Large bodied, Double-crested uniquely exhibits an "Adam's apple" bulge and a bright-orange throat. Immature birds are paler about the head and breast than the black adults.

On the oceanic side, the Pelagic and the Brandt's Cormorant are wedded to salt water. Both nest at the outer point, but have distinctly different designs on housing specifications and so don't compete for real estate. With a lofty view, and one free of predators, pairs of Pelagics cling to sheer cliffs, nesting in small clefts or crannies in the rock face. Brandt's, by contrast, is very gregarious and prefers gentle slopes or rounded crowns of great rocks.

From late spring to fall, Brandt's Cormorants often gather to feed in large, sometimes immense numbers on bait, typically anchovies. Here, they form the nucleus of what then becomes a spectacle. Joining them at the seafood banquet come untold numbers of pelicans, loons, and gulls.

Top to bottom: Double-crested, Brandt's, and Pelagic

Peregrine Falcon

Falco peregrinus
Fairly common—September to April, otherwise uncommon
16″–18″

Earth's fastest creature, once nearly the rarest, prized by falconers for centuries, supremely adroit, nearly globally distributed, fierce defender of nest and young... the superlatives go on.

To appreciate such lofty declarations, however, you must witness this falcon. At Point Reyes, scan the sky, cliff outcrops, and twisted driftwood. Listen for their harsh, unsettling, *SKREEE-CHUK!* call. Always alert, shorebirds tilt their heads sideways and glance skyward. Look in the same direction, and frequently, high overhead, a dot on a clear blue sky—a Peregrine. Discover one of Earth's most celebrated creatures by knowing where, and *how*, to look.

What might a Peregrine's worldly perspective be? Perhaps...

Try to keep up! Ravenous chicks, ALWAYS hungriest predawn. Hunting's been crappy. Try raising a family on two sandpipers and a blackbird a day! Mate's useless. He brought *nothing* yesterday. Wind's howling. I'm outta here. Updraft off lighthouse extraordinary. Flex scapulars, draw wrists, double my speed. Peninsula in view. Bank right, turbulence annuls all other sound. On a taut-line course, Abbotts Lagoon's my target. None of this tacking left or right kestrel bull. The Great Beach is my highway. With this wind, altitude, and momentum, be there rapidly. Sun rising off right wing, thin marine layer off left. Dip slightly, velocity increases. Can't believe luck! Skein of duck, dead ahead. Sight locked on lagging bird. All else a blur.

Flick wingtips thrice. I'm all in. Teal belatedly realizes merciless approach. My balled fists connect, as the hallux slices. Ducks scatter. Gravity takes hold. Limp quarry tumbles to mudflat. Bank sharply, rapid deceleration, land... FAMISHED!

I become a Green-winged Teal, dressed in a Peregrine.

Below: adult (*left*) and juvenile (*right*)

Common Murre

Uria aalge
Common—Resident
17"

Life itself would seem challenging for a Common Murre, even on a good day. A high degree of resilience is demanded from a creature who thrives in a living room of open ocean and considers sea cliffs, pelted by stinging wind, a proper nursery. Garnering the myriad fish and invertebrates necessary to sustain life while providing for a continually famished chick demands much from this sturdy marine bird.

Foraging, typically in pursuit of small fish, murres dive, submarine-like, to great depths through cold inshore waters. Like a penguin using its flippers, murres flap their wings for propulsion. Transporting a crop full of groceries, adults proceed to hungry offspring gathered in great breeding colonies on broad, guano-painted rocks at Point Reyes's tip. On a blur of skinny wings, they fly with the momentum and grace of a well-thrown football. Arriving birds suddenly appear and awkwardly land. Densely packed, many hundreds of doting adults and variously sized chicks jostle, preen, rest, or depart. Picking and weaving through thousands of nesting birds, adults work toward their young for feeding.

Come fledging time, the chicks are about one-quarter the weight of an adult. Young make their way down to the rocky cliff edge and jump or tumble into the roiling sea far below. The buoyant chick is joined by the adult male, who cares for it until it is grown and able to fly.

Eking out a life like this is hard enough. Add the additional burdens wrought by humans—reckless egg theft, oil spills, gill netting, or nesting disturbances—then include the depletion of populations from El Niño's water-warming events, and this supposedly *common* murre starts to seem more like a rough-and-tumble miracle.

Barn Swallow

Hirundo rustica
Common—March to September
6.75"

Some birds have silhouettes that are unmistakable, even iconic. The jazzy Barn Swallow is just such a species. With sweeping lines, greatly elongated tail trains, and gracefully curved wings, it will always be identifiable and never out of style.

In March, Barn Swallows return to Point Reyes after having wintered as far off as South America. Polished glossy blue and warm cinnamon, they zoom and swoop around the farms, barns, and shorelines of the peninsula. Their aerial deftness along with bright chattering calls adds a sense of dynamism to any encounter. Nimble, they pick off flying insects at all elevations. Birds sail high above the Earth, or course just a few inches over the sand.

Shortly after arriving, pairs begin building nests or refurbishing the remains of nests from previous years. The open cup is typically composed of mud and straw and constructed on a stout beam, under a protecting eve. The big old wooden barns at Point Reyes have both of those important components. Also, insects attracted to livestock ensure a ready food supply. Wires offer ample perches; walls and roofs provide shelter. The final element needed—a door left ajar, or a little broken window pane for unbarred access.

There are often other species of swallows sharing this rich habitat, especially the Cliff Swallow. These mud specialists adhere their grapefruit-sized nests, in large clusters, to the undersurfaces of eaves or highway overpasses. Sometimes numbering into the dozens, all these hungry mouths need to be fed. Fortunately, the atmosphere above Point Reyes provides a bill of fare as extensive as the sky. We all benefit from the effective pest control when swallows are here, healthy and hunting.

White-crowned Sparrow

Zonotrichia leucophrys nuttalli
Common—Resident

7"

Some species of birds all appear basically the same throughout their range, at least to us humans, whereas others show patterns of geographic variation such that different breeding populations (known as races, or subspecies) can frequently be distinguished in the field. Sometimes different races occur together in the non-breeding season, as with White-crowns at Point Reyes.

In the fall and winter, differentiating the *nuttalli* White-crowned Sparrow from the visiting *pugatensis* and *gambelli* races depends on subtle color differences. In spring, nearly all sparrows, including White-crowned Sparrow subspecies, depart for more northern and easterly breeding grounds.

In the nesting season, outer Point Reyes plays host to the *nuttalli* White-crowned, found year-round. If you see a White-crowned Sparrow between May and August, hopping among the yellow bush lupine or feeding along trails at the outer point, you are almost certainly regarding a resident *nuttalli* White-crown.

It's logical that, being nonmigratory, *nuttalli* would have shorter wings than those of its migratory cousins. The feathers at the bend of the wrist are yellowish instead of white. The bill is quite dull yellow, rather than pinkish or orange. The crown pattern is somewhat muted, appearing less strikingly black and white than in other races. Birds show a subtle whisker mark, where other races lack one. Their back streaks are blackish brown rather than rusty, and their flanks are extensively brownish, rather than gray-brown, adding to an overall dingier appearance.

The song of the *nuttalli* White-crown is high, thin, and lilting. Lasting about three seconds, it's composed of three or four distinct elements. It begins with a level pleasing tone, then a higher slightly tremulous note, followed by a rapidly vibrating down-slurred quaver.

The Boyds of Summer

See Bird Group Species List for individual species

Summer months see a dramatic reduction in the diversity of bird species found at the point. However, something quite spectacular often takes place during this season. After having nested on exposed, hot, bustling, guano-covered islands in the gulf of Baja, three species referred to as "post-breeding wanderers" arrive en masse to feed in the colder inshore waters of the Point Reyes peninsula. As oceanic upwelling occurs, anchovy numbers bloom. Consequently, Brown Pelicans, Heermann's Gulls, and Elegant Terns detect and greatly profit from the ocean's bounty.

It's an all-you-can-eat buffet as massive feeding flocks turn otherwise calm seas into a chaotic free-for-all with takeout the rule of the day. Plunging from great heights, pelicans, nearly always with an annoying entourage of half a dozen Heermann's Gulls on their tail, do their best to shake off their rear assault. Highly aggressive, these gulls attempt to pilfer wriggling fish from the sides of the pelicans' pouches, overflowing with salt water. Seemingly everywhere, thousands of glittering-white and highly vocal Elegant Terns swarm, hover, and disperse, moving in every direction. Raining into the transparent swells, they pierce the water's surface and momentarily disappear, only to pop back into flight with a tiny wriggling fish they consume with a deft toss into the air. Pods of sea lions patrolling the swirling masses of fish frighten prey to the surface as more aquatic havoc is wrought. The raucous chattering of terns and strained cries of gulls carry far over the calm summer swells as splashing, plunging, and chaos continue.

Whether the massive bait ball disperses or is outright depleted, it's hard to say, but as quickly as the frenzy forms, it vanishes.

Top to bottom: Brown Pelican, Heermann's Gull, Elegant Tern

Western Gull

Larus occidentalis
Common—Resident
25″

Never far from salt water, this is the iconic gull of coastal California. Let's get to know this seaside custodian. An important species with a large presence, the Western Gull is undeniably big, bold, and brash.

Whether town crier or watchman, the Western Gull has astonishingly refined eyesight. The first to alert all other birds to a perceived threat or a predator's presence, they climb quickly skyward on shallow, modified wingbeats. Bellowing deep, husky, and frenzied *ARNK! ARNK! ARNK!* notes, Western Gulls demand the attention of all creatures within earshot. There are certain head-down postures, combined with loud vocalizations, that define personal territory or symbolize individual superiority. Distinct calls communicate intent, threat, or potential food availability.

Males are just slightly larger than females. Young start out as variably mottled brown, progressively becoming whiter as maturity is reached in four years. Adults' heads and bodies are flawless snow white, while the back or mantle is dark slate gray. Often appearing to be the tail, the black wing tips anointed with a white spot at the tip of each feather extend beyond the unmarked white tail. Their yellow bill comes equipped with a bold red spot near the bulbous tip; the legs are bright pink.

Habitats frequented include large swaths of offshore Pacific, sandy beaches, tidal mudflats, lagoons, rock stacks, garbage dumps, or anywhere children throw snacks to endlessly famished gulls. While over a hundred pairs breed on Point Reyes, thousands nest on the nearby Farallon Islands. They seem to have few dietary limitations, gladly consuming soft-bodied worms, crabs, invertebrates, and even oversized starfish. Scavengers, they also benefit from dead fish, birds, and marine mammals.

Townsend's Warbler

Setophaga townsendi
Fairly common—September to May, otherwise rare
5"

Imagine yourself a migratory bird, say a Townsend's Warbler, following your normal route south to winter in the forests of southern Mexico.

By late August, after nesting in a towering fir in southern British Columbia, your four chicks have all fledged. If successful at avoiding predators, pesticides, and power lines, they'll find their way south. You'll likely never see them again. By early September, you arrive in coastal Northern California. Consuming a breakfast of insects, you replace fat used in your previous night's flight. Lastly, you find a secluded locale to bathe, preen, and sleep until dark.

Waking up healthy and restless, you move into the crown of an immense redwood. There you scan cloudless sky, taking in the stars. Getting your bearings straight, you stretch your wings, vocalize . . . and push off. Earth vanishes far below as you climb several hundred feet. Free from its terrestrial embrace, you've no predators. Encompassed by a scintillating dome of stars, your body temperature increases, efficiently utilizing reserves of fat. Call notes from migratory songbirds assure you you're not alone. A cool breeze at your back, half a mile of elevation below your feet, you reach cruising altitude. A natural internal navigation system gives you an innate knowledge of which star clusters guide you to your destination. With street signs written in the stars, you're traveling on an invisible path, used for eons.

As dawn diminishes the Milky Way's clarity, you descend. To your right, endless sea; to your left, land sprinkled with lights, as dairy farmers awaken. Plummeting toward a beacon of light, you locate a stand of twisted cypress, and land safely at the tip of Point Reyes.

Northern Parula

Setophaga americana
Extremely rare—April to October
4.5″

Try to imagine the worldly perspective of a single Northern Parula, a denizen of America's eastern forests. *This* parula, however, is on a different journey because its navigational system is unusual. It's thought that a minute percentage of migrants possess a sort of dyslexia whereby directional compasses are reversed. This can scatter birds far off course.

This voyage begins far south, in Yucatán, a tropical region covered by forest, and an annual migration destination for over one hundred species. Spring dawns, and natural cues trigger a desire to migrate. In April, parulas depart pyramid-studded jungles and fly five hundred miles to Louisiana, Cuba, or Florida.

However, *our* warbler travels eight hundred miles northwest, reaching the Texas coast. In May, it crosses New Mexico's deserts and by June is greeted by a great wall, the Sierra Nevada. Perfectly able, it vaults the crest, drops west over forested slopes, and crosses a great valley. Breeze at its back, it passes west over the Coast Range, paying no heed to the thick clouds below. Descending at dawn, a new reality becomes clear. Our parula looks down on a world . . . without land.

Over surging pewter swells, sky obscured, without directional cues, it meanders. Thankfully, something draws its attention, a pulsing light! Instinct kicks in. Digging at reserves, it tacks left, then swings right, cleaving an irregular but steady path toward an ever-brightening target. Emerging before our ephemeral bird are enormous tortured cliffs, waves, and queer seabird calls. Past the rotating beam it climbs, eager for something approximating plant life. Wearied, our tropical gift crowns the prominent citadel, lowers its delicate yellow feet, and lights on a twisted cypress atop Point Reyes.

Tricolored Blackbird

Agelaius tricolor
Uncommon—February to May
Common—September to October, otherwise rare
8.75"

"Wow! Look at THAT!" These words are likely shouted out by excited families at Point Reyes when first encountering Tricolored Blackbirds. When a well-defined, choreographed blob of, say, one or two thousand black birds suddenly sweeps across the road, visitors tend to perk up. Between barns, on tractors, over muddy stubble, or beneath grazing Holsteins, the seemingly abundant Tricolored Blackbird congregates to feed. This belies the evidence of a disturbing truth: there used to be *many more*.

An essentially California bird, it has witnessed a steady decline, from an estimated two to three million birds in the 1930s down now to perhaps around two hundred thousand. The vast majority breed in California's Central Valley and nearby foothills. They don't nest at Point Reyes, but visit in large numbers, primarily in fall and early winter. Afterward, they disperse for locations often unknown, likely back to Central Valley dairy farms and agricultural lands. They rely on emergent marsh habitat, flooded fields with insects, and grain.

Male Tricolored Blackbirds appear similar in appearance to the widespread Red-winged Blackbird. Tricolored shows a clear and diagnostic white wing band below a darker-red shoulder. They also exhibit a slightly longer bill, wings, and tail, imparting a lankier appearance. Our local Red-winged Blackbird, the "Bicolored," shows only red against the black, no white.

Red-wings may breed in large colonies; however, the Tricolored forms the greatest breeding congregation of any songbird known in North America, literally into the thousands. While difficult to adequately describe, the "grinding buzz-saw" or "cat in heat" song of a male Tricolored is most memorable. The outpouring from hundreds or potentially thousands is truly remarkable.

In flight: female (*left*) and male (*right*)

Red-tailed Hawk

Buteo jamaicensis
Common—Resident
19″–22″

The Red-tailed Hawk is a big bird with a large presence at Point Reyes. Coming in several "flavors" here in the West, the majority are considered light Red-tails; adults are buff below, juveniles whitish with a speckled cummerbund. Look at plenty and you'll encounter intermediate and dark individuals with reddish or blackish brown bodies. Red-tailed Hawks may be the most variable bird species in North America.

With an abundance of small mammals, Point Reyes hosts many birds of prey. Visit the outer point in fall, and the numbers of resting, foraging, or migrating hawks can be impressive. Southbound raptors who keep the Pacific to their right and land on their left will stay on the coast. Consequently, hawks find themselves "running out of land" when they reach the tip of Point Reyes.

Raptors such as vultures, eagles, and several buteos, including the Red-tail, have a strong aversion to flying over open ocean. Eventually they execute a U-turn, go northeast, and then continue south. Others, such as falcons and osprey, frequently venture offshore.

Autumn on Point Reyes is warm, and one thing all birds of prey seek is a good-old thermal. Rising columns of heated air afford raptors lift, an elevator ride to the top floor of any invisible skyscraper towering over sun-soaked earth. These conditions lubricate the wheels of raptor migration. Effortlessly garnering height benefits traveling predators, allowing soaring birds to repeatedly ascend and to progress on their journey, frequently free from flapping. These altitudes provide unparalleled views for sharp-eyed predators.

Thermals can contain numerous species in migration. Look first at the top and work down, as eagles tend to rise quicker than others and thereby crown the warmth.

Western Bluebird

Sialia mexicana
Common—Resident
7"

Yellow-rumped Warbler

Setophaga coronata auduboni
Common—September to May
5.5"

As the saying goes, "Birds of a feather flock together." Well . . . not always! Different species of birds frequently find each other's company suitable. Shorebirds of all stripes "bump elbows" on the mudflat, and ducks of every dimension come eye to eye at the pond's mirrored surface. However, few species seem to purposely go out of their way to associate or even forage with a conspicuously different species—one from a different family to boot! A feeling of gladness passes over me each time I encounter the inclusive relationship between the Western Bluebird and Yellow-rumped Warbler.

Come October, most warblers have long departed for southern tropical haunts; our companion, however, formerly known as the Audubon's Warbler, chooses to winter in California. Butter Butts, as they're lovingly called, often form large foraging flocks that can number into the dozens, an unusual trait for most warblers.

The vast majority of warblers inhabit trees; however, these aerialists frequently move from forested areas and gather in loose assemblages to feed in open terrain. Communicating with soft, dry "chip notes," Yellow-rumps are unfailingly neighborly with another kindly bird, the Western Bluebird. Whether they profit from the larger bluebird scaring up insects or simply benefit from more watchful eyes, all prosper. Late breakfast or early supper, meals are garnered from the wide-open spaces of Point Reyes. Here they feed from coyote brush dining tables with dairy-farm barbed-wire seating. It's an all-you-can-eat buffet in a spread of lupine, as active parties gather and glean all manner of insect life.

Butter Butts and bluebirds are typically at ease around humans, allowing close viewing of the subtle variations in their exquisite plumages.

Companionship. It's a beautiful thing!

American Kestrel

Falco sparverius
Common—October to March, otherwise uncommon
9″–10.5″

All-American bird! Sharing Earth with such a lovely, interesting, and dynamic creature is for me a gift of the greatest kind. Ranging from California to Maine, Alaska to Chile, the widely cherished American Kestrel has a true fan base. What is it about this little falcon that holds our attention and admiration? It might be the overall package. Before all else, this bird arrives to any event dressed in a stunning color-coordinated motif. Expressive whiskers, snappy cap, and anointing spots dress each bird. Sexual differences are striking. Females are larger and boldly tiger-striped above in black and rust.

A one-bird squadron, the kestrel is beyond fearless. Pugnacious, these birds bravely strafe Golden Eagles, usher Red-tails to more serene environs, and convince Great Horned Owls . . . you know, otherwise!

Hunting for mouse or cricket, this small predator is able to hover motionless for many moments on narrow pointed pinwheel-like wings. Slightly meandering, kestrels progress with deep, rapid, cleaving wingbeats. Landing, kestrels pump their tails and repeatedly bob their heads in an exaggerated fashion, appearing momentarily off balance. The call is a ringing, slightly frantic, *Kil-LEE!, Kil-LEE!, Kil-LEE!* that often turns your head.

In the nonbreeding season, kestrels are numerous on the outer point, and females are far more plentiful than males. Larger, they likely outcompete smaller males, thereby dominating the rodent-rich outer point. From telephone wires, or soaring high above, they stare down into rolling grassland. Scarce, sporadic, or absent as breeders on Point Reyes, most Marin birds breed east of the fault line where oaks with old Northern Flicker holes provide perfect nurseries. Nest box–building volunteers lovingly create homes for kestrels to breed, and I thank them!

59

Shorebirds of Point Reyes

See Bird Group Species List for individual species

The term *shorebird* doesn't simply apply to every bird found at the shore. Gulls, terns, and herons all live at the shore, but are not considered shorebirds. "Shorebird" is loosely used as a large umbrella that encompasses four families and multiple genera. There are roughly thirty species of sandpipers one could hope to encounter at Point Reyes in an average year, including oyster-catcher, plover, sandpiper, godwit, and snipe, to name a few.

One of the most interesting aspects of shorebirds is how their sizes range from diminutive to considerable. There's a gradual "stair-step" in sizes that exists from the Least Sandpiper at the small end, to a bird thirty times its weight, the Long-billed Curlew, at the other. Also fascinating is the variation in bill structures. Shorebirds' bills differ in length, width, and depth. Some are curved, others recurved, straight, blunt, delicate, or compressed. These various shapes, lengths, and forms function to meet each species' requirements for garnering the diversity of invertebrates they consume for their survival.

Consequently, many different species can all forage together and not compete. They're gathering different prey items that occur at different depths on or under the soil, sand, or mud. Sanderlings chase waves and pick sand fleas from the surface. Curlews, Whimbrels, and godwits plunge their bills up to their faces to reach deep for Ghost Shrimp. Snowy Plovers run, stop, and pick from the surface. Turnstones do just that, while Surf-birds and oystercatchers fly in between crashing waves to quickly seize prey. Dowitchers, Dunlin, and small sandpipers probe into mud, feeling for invertebrates with sensitive bills, while phala-ropes scissor organisms upward using capillary action.

Sandpiper bills ... nature's tool chest.

Top to bottom: Long-billed Curlew, Marbled Godwit, Wilson's Snipe, Semipalmated Plover, Sanderling, and Least Sandpiper

Great Horned Owl

Bubo virginianus
Common—Resident
22″

You know those moments when night's darkness draws close and you ever-so-scarcely perceive a form brushed by the soft edge of your low beams? Quickly floating up from ground or fencepost, it vanishes. Neck hairs tingle. Was it your imagination, exhaustion catching up with you, or, perhaps... an owl?

The numerous small groves of conifers dotting the peninsula provide exceptional cover for a nocturnal predator, the Great Horned Owl. Perched motionless in daylight, they're cloaked in cryptic fall colors and shaped like a small wine barrel with a bowling ball for a head. At other times, this robust, full-bodied, and awe-inspiring predator appears as an extremely alert feline.

Conversely, Great Horns can also emanate drowsy disregard as they gaze down through narrowed eyes, set deep within a smoothly swiveling turret. This look of calm passivity is deceptive, because this isn't a creature to exchange friendly glances with if you're, say, smaller than an adult Surf Scoter.

Just imagine. At feeding time, these three-pound carnivores lean forward into the darkness, open broad, rounded wings, and drop from the high crowns of conifers. Gliding, they silently descend, gather momentum, and continue out and over the waters of Drakes Bay. Locating sleeping scoters, a hunting owl will zero in on an individual and seize it. Hoisting up a sea duck two-thirds its own weight from the Pacific's rolling surface takes considerable strength. Rising with prey, these great owls climb a few hundred feet in altitude and return to the cypresses.

Whether of grebe, Burrowing Owl, Red-throated Loon, or scoter, the various wings littering the Earth beneath these trees give testament to this apex predator's strength and capabilities.

Rock Wren

Salpinctes obsoletus
Uncommon—Resident
6"

A subtle yet unique feature of this bird is that it typically avoids assuming the iconic "cocked tail" stance of most wren species. It prefers to carry its buffy-tipped tail close to the rocks from which it sings.

Not a bird encountered and beheld by the masses, Rock Wrens are distinctive, peculiar, and certainly well worth getting to know. Abundant nowhere, they occur at Point Reyes, but are easily missed. Aptly named, Rock Wrens are denizens of boulder, cliff, and slag.

There may be but a small handful of these covert caretakers on the outer point; it's hard to say. These insectivores probe and poke about in close, dark, webby, sodden spaces where few if any *Homo sapiens* have ventured. Much of the Rock Wren's world will forever remain a delightful mystery. Watch for a small, lone brownish-gray bird flying very low and usually short distances. Employing rocks as cover, they pick their way between massive slabs.

Although inconspicuous, these performers pour forth sweet auditory rivulets, ringing trills, and diverse riffs that cascade and tumble down the steep, tortured strata of Point Reyes's colossal face. What better stage could there possibly be than the weather-battered, wind-whipped, water-scoured tip of Point Reyes? Here, wrens take their rightful place, jewel-like, atop the crowning promontory of the greatest rock about, and sing their hearts out for all the world to hear.

Singing males will usually alight on a prominent spire, repeatedly bow, bob, and every few seconds toss back their head and perform. Their chests swell, pouring forth songs, trills, and creative arrangements, with few phrases repeated. Some vocalizations seem more like experiments in capability, quality, or mimicry than song.

Bird Group Species List

In addition to the unique life history of each species, there are also inter-esting groupings, relationships, and events that enhance any day spent afield at Point Reyes. See more details at the page numbers listed below.

Sparrows of Point Reyes (see page 14)

The following species are common—fall, winter, and spring. Song and White-crowned are resident.

> Savannah Sparrow—*Passerculus sandwichensis* – 5.5"
> Song Sparrow—*Melospiza melodia* – 6.25"
> Lincoln's Sparrow—*Melospiza lincolnii* – 5.75"
> White-crowned Sparrow—*Zonotrichia leucophrys* – 7"
> Golden-crowned Sparrow—*Zonotrichia atricapilla* – 7.25"
> Fox Sparrow—*Passerella iliaca* – 7"

Point Reyes Spring Seabird Migration (see page 26)

Commonality status refers to spring only.

> Pacific Loon—*Gavia pacifica* – Common, 25"
> Common Murre—*Uria aalge* – Common, 17.5"
> Western Grebe—*Aechmophorus occidentalis* – Common, 25"
> Clark's Grebe—*Aechmophorus clarkii* – Uncommon 25"
> Eared Grebe—*Podiceps nigricollis* – Uncommon, 13"
> Horned Grebe—*Podiceps auritus* – Uncommon, 14"
> Red-necked Grebe—*Podiceps grisegena* – Rare, 18"
> Brant—*Branta bernicla* – Common, 25"
> Pigeon Guillemot—*Cepphus columba* – Common, 13.5"
> White-winged Scoter—*Melanitta deglandi* – Rare, 21"
> Harlequin Duck—*Histrionicus histrionicus* – Rare, 16.5"

Double-crested, Brandt's, and Pelagic Cormorants (see page 34)

All common and resident.

> Double-crested Cormorant—*Nannopterum auritum* – 33"
> Brandt's Cormorant—*Urile penicillatus* – 34"
> Pelagic Cormorant—*Urile pelagicus* – 28"

The Boyds of Summer (see page 44)

Commonality and seasonality information appears below.

> Brown Pelican—*Pelecanus occidentalis* – Common May to October, otherwise uncommon, 50"
> Heermann's Gull—*Larus heermanni* – Common July to November, otherwise rare, 19"
> Elegant Tern—*Thalasseus elegans* – Common August to September, otherwise rare, 17"

Shorebirds of Point Reyes (see page 60)

Shorebirds are diverse in size, shape, and seasonality. Some, such as Killdeer and Black Oystercatcher, are resident, found all year. Many highly migratory species occur here in spring and fall, while others fit somewhere in between.

> Killdeer—*Charadrius vociferus* – 10.5"
> Whimbrel—*Numenius phaeopus* – 17.5"
> Wilson's Snipe—*Gallinago delicata* – 10.5"
> Least Sandpiper—*Calidris minutilla* – 6"
> Long-billed Curlew—*Numenius americanus* – 23"
> Sanderling—*Calidris alba* – 8"
> Marbled Godwit—*Limosa fedoa* – 18"
> Snowy Plover—*Charadrius nivosus* – 6.25"
> Black Turnstone—*Arenaria melanocephala* – 9.25"
> Surfbird—*Calidris virgata* – 10"
> Black Oystercatcher—*Haematopus bachmani* – 17.5"
> Dunlin—*Calidris alpina* – 8.5"
> Long-billed Dowitcher—*Limnodromus scolopaceus* – 11.5"
> Red-necked Phalarope—*Phalaropus lobatus* – 7.75"

Acknowledgments

The concept for this book began squarely with Steve Wasserman, Heyday's publisher. Always having clicked creatively, we fashioned inspirational ideas focusing on the birds of Point Reyes. I immediately understood his concept, shared his vision, and went straight to work.

While writing the species accounts (and after), I had the great privilege of working closely with Heyday's crew of knowledgeable, talented, patient, and unfailingly friendly professionals. A delight to create with, these skilled craftspeople taught me much. They make me look good! They are Heyday's acquisitions editor, Marthine Satris; the copyeditor, Michele Jones; the managing editor, Emmerich Anklam; the art director, Diane Lee; the production manager, Marlon Rigel; the marketing and publicity manager, Kalie Caetano; and the sales manager, Chris Carosi. Thank you one . . . and all.

To Patricia, the love of my life. Thank you for being my honest sounding board, my contiguous reviewer, and my forever partner. Once again, this book would never have been possible without your love and companionship.

A heartfelt thanks goes to one of my dearest friends, Steve Howell, for his generous help with this book. Coming to any book project, he brings not only decades of experience of things avian but also a deep love and reverence for words. Whether through devilish pun, clever limerick, or mastery of using the fewest words to say more than thought possible, he is a gifted artisan of language.

To my friend Adam Donkin, who helped from the sidelines with a myriad of elements and was involved with much of the "vibe" of this book. Adam graciously bestowed his thoughtful and creative ideas whenever possible, be they instructive, structural, or artistic.

To all my friends over the many years who have shared their knowledge, time, and companionship exploring Point Reyes, I thank you deeply! Whether we were peering into the magical nooks and crannies of this stunningly beautiful peninsula, dashing to witness the next feathered waif, or gazing far out to sea in search of oceanic glory, these personal experiences, punctuated by thrilling sightings, have influenced every element of this book.

Finally, with the deepest love a person can feel for a place, I thank Point Reyes itself. Bold in form, rock solid in substance, sweeping in scope, magical in character, inspiring in beauty, and life-brimming in reality, I am blessed to have spent much of my life with you.

About the Author

Keith Hansen authored and illustrated *Hansen's Field Guide to the Birds of the Sierra Nevada* (Heyday, 2021), a field guide companion to *Birds of the Sierra Nevada: Their Natural History, Status, and Distribution*. He is a professional bird illustrator whose images have been featured in *Discovering Sierra Birds*; *Birds of Yosemite and the East Slope*; and *Natural History of the Point Reyes Peninsula*, among other books.